Little Inventors Go Green!

Inventing for a better planet

by Katherine Mengardon
and Dominic Wilcox

Credits

Words **Katherine Mengardon**
Drawings **Dominic Wilcox**
Design **Jack Clarke***

Publisher **Michelle l'Anson**
Editors
Sarah Woods
Karen Midgley

With help from our Little Inventors team
Will Evans, Chelsea Vivash, Emilie Harrak, Jill Bennison,
Suzy O'Hara, Gareth Lloyd

Our always ingenious Little Inventors, Magnificent Makers
and brilliant partners across the world.

With a special thank you to Nick, Natacha and Rudy Coates,
Justine Boussard, Ruby and Sally O'Hara, Leila Harrak, Max
and Maggie Evans, Holly and Maya Mataric.

Real inventions in the book include: WaterSeer by VICI-
Labs, Ocean Cleanup by Boyan Slat, Air-Ink by Graviky
Labs, air pollution jewellery by Studio Dan Roosegaarde,
Singapore's Man Made Trees by Grants Associates.

Little Inventors® is a registered trademark of
Little Inventors Worldwide Ltd.

* Based on an original design by **Naomi (Atkinson) White**

Published by Collins
An imprint of HarperCollins Publishers
Westerhill Road, Bishopbriggs,
Glasgow G64 2QT
www.harpercollins.co.uk
© HarperCollins Publishers 2020

A catalogue record for this book is available from the
British Library.

Printed and bound in China by
RR Donnelley APS Co Ltd

ISBN 978-0-00-838289-6

10 9 8 7 6 5 4 3 2 1

*" There are four million different kinds of animals
and plants in the world. That's four million solutions
to the problem of staying alive. "*

David Attenborough

Chapter 1

Little Inventors go green...

Inventing for a better planet

What is Little Inventors?

We are a team that believes children like you have the best ideas, and that they can change the world.

Over 10,000 children from all over the world have already sent us their invention drawings, and over 250 of them have been chosen to be made real!

Professional artists, designers and makers help us bring the most ingenious ideas to life, through objects, animations or 3D models.

Arthur, age 8, invented the Super Grow 11000.

He was one of thirteen Little Inventors at the **Great Exhibition of the North** in Newcastle in summer 2018 **and** even appeared on his favourite TV show, Gardeners' World.

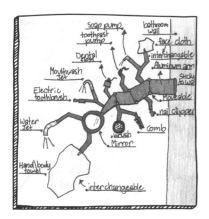

It's a mini version of the Canadarm on the International Space Station. It holds bathroom items needed by astronauts, to stop them from floating away.

Amy was one of the winners of the **Inventions for Space challenge** and her invention travelled to the International Space Station!!

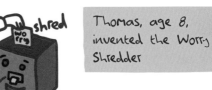

Thomas, age 8, invented the Worry Shredder

" It shreds worries and prints out solutions and gives you a chocolate."

Thomas won the global **Future as big as your imagination challenge** and travelled to Sharjah to see his invention in an amazing exhibition!

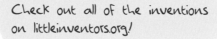

Check out all of the inventions on littleinventors.org!

The journey of invention

Every object that you see was invented by someone. Someone who was once a child just like you.

A child just like you who had **an idea.**

An idea that came from looking around and noticing things.

Things that could be better, easier or just more fun.

And the best bit is to take an idea as far as you can and make it into a real invention...

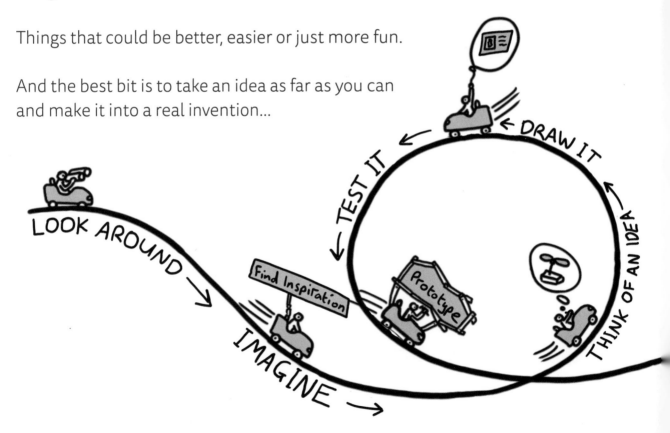

You are a born inventor

...everyone is!

From the moment you are born, you start figuring out the world. You have to learn to eat, to speak, to walk, to play and to have fun! And as you do that, you get to discover everything for the first time.

Being curious is the most natural thing for humans.

That's how we learn to adapt to our environment.

When you see new things, your brain records all sorts of information. Then it needs to ask questions to put them in order, so it can use the information later for different things, like **solving problems.**

And this is where new ideas are happiest.

Curious children ask up to 93 questions a day!!
We bet you have some questions of your own....

With your discovering head on, it's time to put your natural talents to work!

And what better place to start than with nature itself?

Chapter 2

Nature is the true mother of invention...

Go wild and get inventing

Nature is all around us and has been for millions of years.

In fact, it was there a long time before us. And of course, nature invented humans too!

Look up and try to catch a glimpse of nature right now. It might be a tree, a flower, a fly or a cloud in the sky.

Each of these was created by nature, **finding ways to solve problems...**

Plants invented flowers to attract insects to help them scatter their pollen.

Squids have developed black ink to hide behind when under attack!

Hermit crabs use seashells as homes and move to bigger shells when they outgrow them!

In fact, every living thing is constantly changing to find the perfect attributes to survive in its own environment.

Evolution is invention in very slow motion!

Planet Earth: our home

Earth happened to be in the right place at the right time. The right distance from the sun, the right amount of water and the right atmosphere have led to life sprouting on Earth. It's the only planet in the whole galaxy with life on it... that we know of!

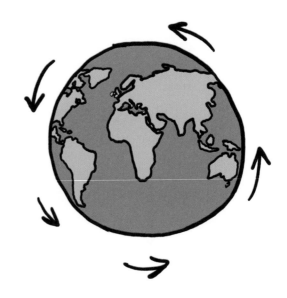

And what life!
From deserts to forests, oceans to mountains, our planet is home to the most amazing creatures and plants, a constant source of wonder for us.

But like all homes, we need to take care of it! Everything is connected in a very fine balance – and this can be upset by what we do.

Scientists all agree: we have to change how we live so we can take better care of our planet.

Nature is all around us, in cities just as in the countryside, and what each of us does matters...

And this is where **YOU** come in. We need to start having better ideas on how to enjoy nature and take more care of it, now.

So how about taking a good look at the natural world to inspire you?

Inspired by nature

There is so much creativity in nature that we humans have learnt a lot from copying plants and animals...

Burdock plant

velcro

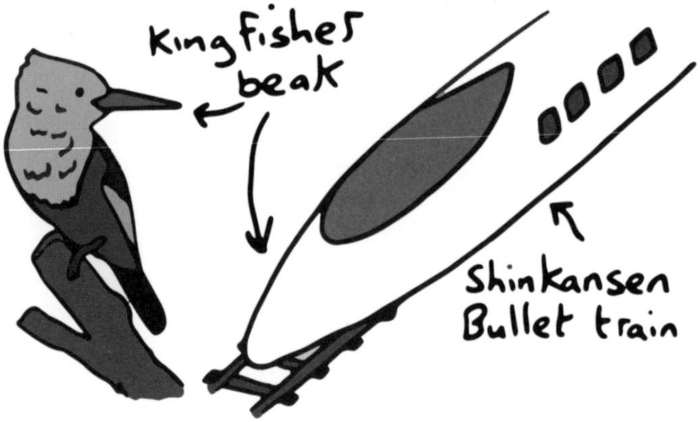

Kingfisher beak

Shinkansen Bullet train

Octopus

suckers

Sonar

Dolphin

Submarine

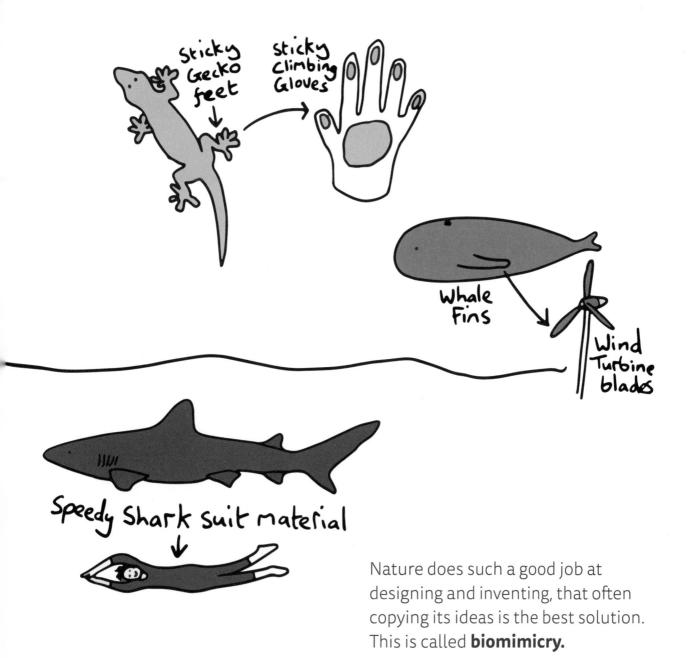

Nature does such a good job at designing and inventing, that often copying its ideas is the best solution. This is called **biomimicry.**

Your invention journey to make the world a greener place

This book will give you lots of ideas for things to explore and think up, with ingenious invention ideas that can help make our planet a better, greener, healthier and more fun place to live.

Creatures!

Trash talk!

Move it!

Power up!

Come rain or come shine!

Oakay-dokey!

Go green!

With a little help from our **Chief Inventor Dominic Wilcox...**

The plant pot umbrella

Now that's a great way to enjoy the rain and be a little greener every day!

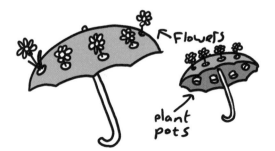

© photo by *Pec studio*

Top inventing tips from our Chief Inventor Dominic!

Follow that thought!

Try to stop thinking for a minute. It's pretty much impossible!

Our brains are constantly taking information in and working out how to record it and how it connects with other things we know.

So trust your brain and try to catch a thought and see where it takes you!

Who needs your help?

Thinking about who your invention is for is a great place to start. It could be for someone in your family or an animal you spot while you're out and about. Imagine what they like, dislike, what they might find difficult or boring – how can you help them?

Share your invention ideas with me on littleinventors.org to get feedback!

No problem too small!

It might be how to help a snail go faster, how to water a cactus, or how to protect a ladybird from the rain – no problem is too small to capture your inventive imagination!

No limits!

And of course, the opposite is also true – there is no problem too big to have a go at either! If you worry about how to reduce the pollution in the atmosphere or how to make travel faster, safer and non-polluting, then have a go. We need all kinds of ideas to help our planet stay green!

What might seem impossible today could well happen in the not-so-distant future.

Break the rules

New inventions happen when we try to think or do things differently – in other words, when we break the rules. So forget how things are supposed to work and make it happen your own way!

What kind of green inventor are you?

Uncover what kind of green inventor you really are!

Your favourite creatures, beasties or other creepy crawlies

Five nature things you love the most on our planet

Your green inventor name

Your first name + Your 1st favourite creature + 2nd best loved thing

Five examples of nature around you

Five things that are bad for nature and the environment

Five things in nature or the environment that you would like to help

Now that you have your green hat firmly on, it's time to get inventing for a greener planet!

Chapter 3

Super furry fishy crawly animals...

All creatures great and small

Wherever you are, you can be sure there are many living creatures close by. It might be a mosquito-eating spider on the ground, a squirrel running along a wall, a frog in a pond, a ladybird on a window or a bird flying overhead...

Wildlife is all around us!

All these bugs, mammals, birds, fish, reptiles and amphibians have a part to play to keep our environment working as it should.

They are just as important as we are!

Creature comforts

Every creature helps to keep nature in balance, by eating (and sometimes being eaten!) and by spreading seeds and pollen. But they also have incredible talents that we can learn from!

Bat wings are actually really flexible hands that make them better at flying than birds. Bats are more closely related to humans than to mice!

Hi Five!

Only mammal that can fly!

Schools of fish use swimming in large groups as a way of saving energy, because swimming together affects the flow of water between them!

Fishy School

Spiders produce up to eight different types of silk, which they can use to make their nests, to hunt, travel or protect themselves, or even to 'fish' for insects! It can be stronger than steel.

Spider silk was used to make bandages and painting canvasses!

Seabirds' poo (guano) makes brilliant food for seaweed. This seaweed helps coral reefs to grow stronger!

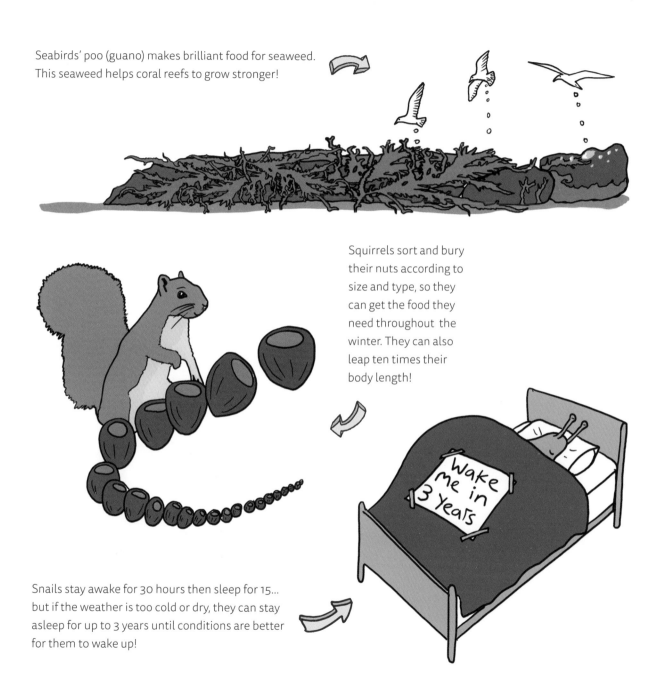

Squirrels sort and bury their nuts according to size and type, so they can get the food they need throughout the winter. They can also leap ten times their body length!

Snails stay awake for 30 hours then sleep for 15... but if the weather is too cold or dry, they can stay asleep for up to 3 years until conditions are better for them to wake up!

Go wild for wildlife!

Wildlife is a huge part of the natural world, and the more that mammals, insects, amphibians, birds and other invertebrates thrive, the better for the planet. So it's worth thinking about how **to help and encourage wildlife** in small and big ways.

Plants, trees, flowers and bushes are all instant homes for wildlife, so the more nature the better!

Hedgehogs find it hard to travel from garden to garden because of fences, walls and roads.

Even the smallest creatures need a drink sometimes. Creating a water feature in your garden or school is a great way to help wildlife.

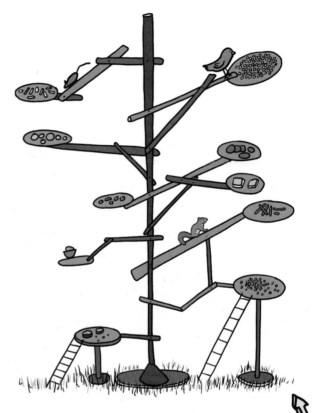

Leave some food out to encourage visitors! But make sure you research the best foods for different animals.

The simplest and most important thing you can do is **enjoy nature** as it is, or help it!!

We all need a roof over our heads...

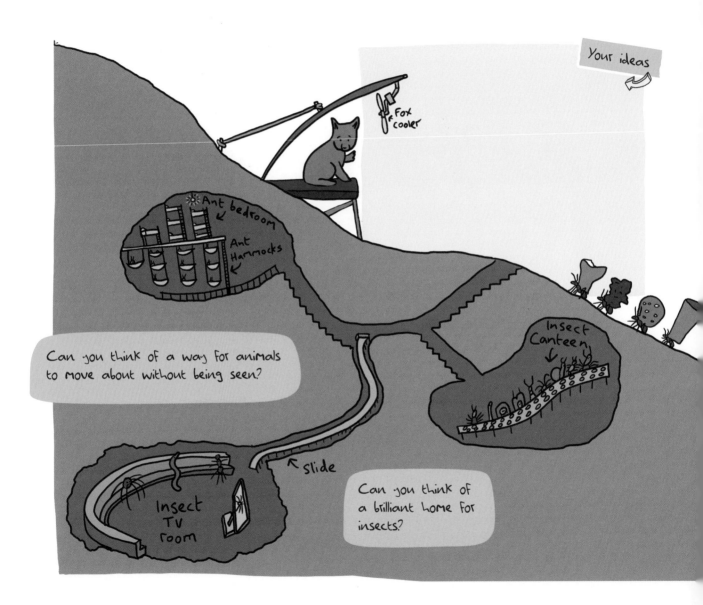

...and we all have places to be!

Breathe life into your invention!

Choose a creature to invent for! Where does it live?
What does it do? What does it need help with?

My creature inspiration

Put yourself in someone else's shoes, paws or claws... and try to see the world through their eyes. You'll be in for a surprise!

Name it!

How it works

MY INVENTION

Draw BIG, use colours and add labels!

Now share it on littleinventors.org!

Inventing can really give you wings!

Animal Friend Badge

There is so much we can learn from our fellow critters and creatures. They can do extraordinary things that most superheroes wouldn't even dream of!

Every ant, slug, ladybird or frog that you may be lucky enough to spot is a little stroke of **nature's genius**, and is worth appreciating fully.

By looking after all creatures great and small, we are taking care of our own world and protecting its precious balance.

From the minds of our Little Inventors...

Snail and turtle sail

Lilo, age 7
Yverdon-les-Bains, Switzerland

Lilo's invention was brought to life by our Magnificent Maker **Lorène Martin**, a costume-making seamstress from the town of Champagne in Switzerland!

...to the skills of our Magnificent Makers

Definitely not a real snail either...

Not a real turtle!

"*Meeting Lilo was a beautiful moment! I really wanted her to be fully involved in the creation of her invention. I know from my job that ideas often change when you start making something. We discussed her idea, and we chose the materials together. Lilo even designed the embroidery pattern for the sail. We even did a radio interview which was really special! I do hope we meet again, she is very talented!*"

Watch me now!

© photo by *le castrum*

Chapter 4

Bin it like you mean it...

Pick of the litter

As you walk down the street, around your playground, or in the middle of nowhere, there is sadly something you are always likely to find... not just nature and creatures but...

We live in a man-made world where everything is wrapped or carried in glass, aluminium, paper, cardboard or plastics of many kinds.

If we think about rubbish as something important and use a little imagination, we can **reduce or reuse** what we throw away.

What goes around...
doesn't always come
back around

The thing is that all of these materials
do come from nature.

Paper and cardboard are
made from trees

Aluminium comes from rocks
in the ground

Plastic is made from
crude oil or plants
like corn

Glass is made using ordinary sand
that we find on beaches

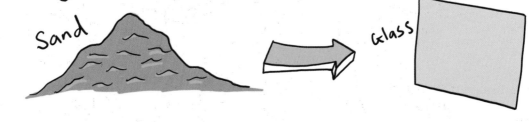

But the way we **process** these materials means that it's
hard for them to get back to their natural state.

So where do they end up? If they are lucky they might end up being recycled, but most of our rubbish ends up in **landfill or in the oceans.**

We throw away about our own body weight in waste every seven weeks!

Glass Tins Plastic

The waste in landfill uses a lot of land and is still just a big pile of smelly rubbish that can be toxic!

Recycling is hugely important in reducing the amount of rubbish that goes into landfill, but sorting items is difficult and time-consuming. It can be confusing to know what to put where.

That's completely bananas!

About one third of food is wasted every year. And a lot of that is fruit and vegetables, but also bread, dairy products and fizzy drinks. Some of it is food waste we can't eat, like banana peel.

8 tonnes or 8,000 kgs!

We eat 274 million bananas every day worldwide and throw away the banana peel.

That's about the same weight in banana peel as 2,055 Tyrannosaurus rex – every single day!

Or 750,075 T. rex of banana peel in one year!!!

Takes up to two years to decompose

The good news is that food waste like banana peel can be recycled to produce energy or turned into fertiliser to grow more food!

Meanwhile, a plastic bottle might take... 450 years to decompose.

We throw away a million plastic bottles a minute. That's about the weight of almost two T. rex every minute!!

...or 120 T. rex every hour,

...or 2,880 every day,

...or more than a million in a year.

Only 14% of all plastic gets recycled each year – that's an awful lot of plastic that ends up in landfill and in the oceans!

Water bottle: 15g
Estimated weight!

Paper makes up 40% of all rubbish!
One tonne of recyclable paper would save cutting down seventeen trees.

Recycle Me!

Reuse, repeat, reuse, repeat

It's said that **99% of everything** we buy goes into the bin within six months. Recycling is a good idea, but in reality only a small amount of trash gets truly recycled.

What we really need is to find a way to use a lot less man-made material and to reuse everything a lot more.

It can start with **shopping power!** Buying products with less or no packaging, buying second-hand clothes, choosing reusable rather than disposable products, borrowing things you need from friends...

Fix it cafes are popping up all over the place – bring broken things and get them repaired!

And nature is always there to inspire us...

List things you use
only once before
throwing them away

Birds are fantastic recyclers and use all sorts
of things they find to build their nests -
what could we reuse to build a home?

Octopus sometimes carry coconut shells to
shield themselves when far from their homes!

What could we carry with us?

Natural recyclers: worms, mushrooms, snails and microbes all help to decompose
matter and speed up the recycling process in nature, and they get a nice meal while
they're doing it!

Have an idea? No time to waste!

Think about ways to use less, reuse or recycle!

Chief Inventor

My waste inspiration

You can start from an existing idea, and build on it. You could bring two things together too - that's another way to recycle!

My Invention!

Name it!

_____

How it works

My Invention

Draw BIG, use colours and add labels!

Now share it on littleinventors.org!

Boom, now that's how to talk rubbish!

We all need to keep **talking rubbish,** to make our world a better place.

Rubbish can be used to create energy or it can be recycled better. And in the future, we might not even have any rubbish at all, as science creates new environment-friendly materials or better ways to break down plastic and other waste.

Meanwhile, we definitely need more ingenious ideas to change how we deal with rubbish, first to create less of it and then to be really clever with what's left!

From the minds of our Little Inventors...

The alarm cup

Rumaan, age 11
Gratsby, UK

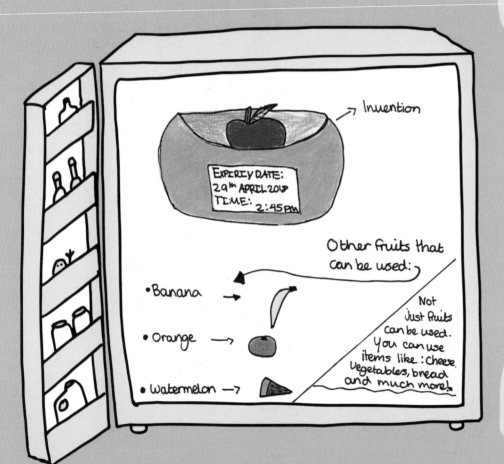

You know how fruit can go all soft and wrinkly if you leave it out in the fruit bowl for too long? Well, no longer!

"The alarm cup is a device that you use to prevent your food from expiring. You place your item in the container and set the alarm for the day that it expires. The alarm will ring two days before the date so that you have enough time to eat or use it."

Rumaan was the winner of our Little Inventors food waste challenge!

...to the skills of our Magnificent Makers

Rumaan's idea was brought to life by Chief Inventor **Dominic Wilcox** and ceramicist **Donnas Peterson:**

Dominic: *"The alarm cup is a ceramic bowl where fruits sit on a little platform with holes to allow air to circulate. It has a device with an inbuilt app where you can program the expiry date of the fruit. What an ingenious and effective idea! "*

Chapter 5

Up, down, far or near...

Go your own way

We like to move it, move it!

Walking, running, driving, cycling, scootering, sailing, flying...
People can't seem to ever stay still!

While we may have two perfectly good feet, more often than not we like **a little help** to get us to other places, near or far.

We travel to be with our families or friends

We go out every day to school or work or shops

We travel to get stuff!!

...or to have fun

To go on holiday

...or because we want to
discover the world

The greenest way to go

The way we travel really matters...

Sailing hardly creates any pollution

There are close to 10,000 planes flying at any given time across the world

The average car trip is less than 20 km long, and by one person with no passengers

Future cars will be driverless

A stained glass driverless car by our chief inventor.

Cycling is three times faster than walking

It would take 346 days to walk non-stop around the Earth

The shape of things to come!

Nature has already inspired so many travel inventions...

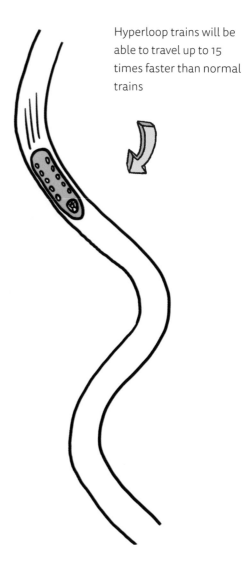

Hyperloop trains will be able to travel up to 15 times faster than normal trains

Vehicles might run on hydrogen, steam or even the kinetic energy they produce!

One thing is for sure, it will be **green energy.**

What other animals could inspire inventions?

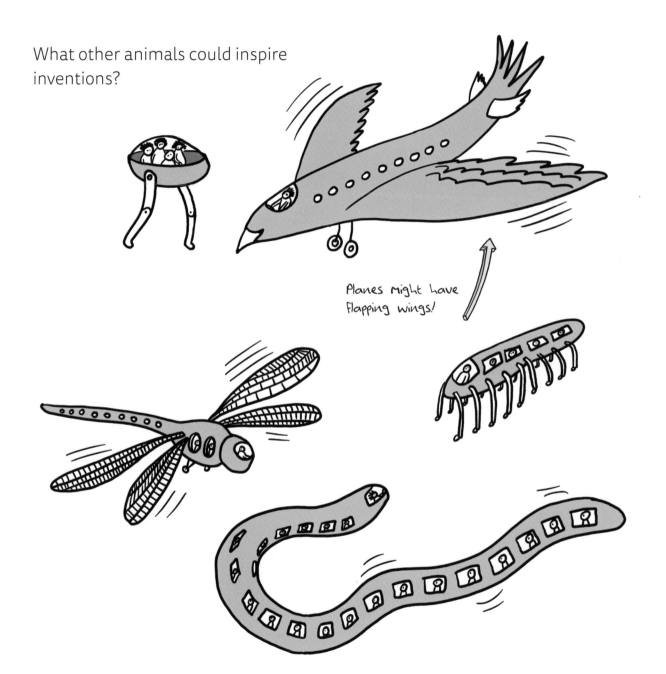

Planes might have flapping wings!

River deep, mountain high

It's not just how you get somewhere, it's where you go! What do you need to think about when you're planning **your next adventure?**

How would you reach the top?

How would you go deep underwater?

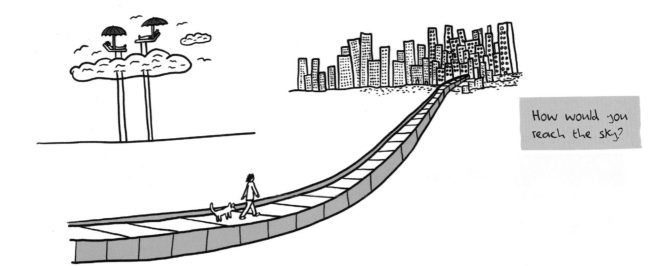

How would you
reach the sky?

How would you travel
with lots of people?

Get your invention idea on track!

We want to keep going to places and for that we need great ideas on how to travel but still be kind to our world. Think about where you want to go and who is going on your trip.

Let your mind travel too. There are no boundaries to how far your imagination can take you!

My travel inspiration

My Invention!

Name it!

How it works

My Invention

Draw BIG, use colours and add labels!

Now share it on littleinventors.org!

Oh! The places you'll go!!

Our everyday lives are full of travel, big and small. It's not only how we live, but it's also how we are part of our world.

It can help us see new things and appreciate our planet. We just need to do it in a way that **respects** our environment!

From the minds of our Little Inventors...

The miracle chair

Sahila, age 12
Sharjah, UAE

" This is a chair designed for the disabled with wings that helps to fly away from the crowds, cars, stairs and buses.

" A disabled person can easily move from place to place. "

Sahila was one of the winners of our **Future as big as your imagination challenge** for the 6th Sharjah Children Biennial, an international celebration of children's art!

The miracle chair was made real by **Sarah Alagroobi,** a multi-discipline artist from the United Arab Emirates.

"The miracle chair drew attention to a part of our lives that we often take for granted – the ability to walk. It showed Sahila's compassion and awareness to those who are less able. It makes the wheelchair a positive symbol for those who dare to dream!

"We used a real wheelchair and added extending multicoloured wings that were stitched by hand. It was such an enjoyable project, it would make anyone want to spread their wings and fly. "

Chapter 6

Is steam coming out of your ears yet?

You've got the power

Scientists all agree...

The way we produce and use **energy** is the biggest reason for pollution on Earth. It's the main cause of climate change.

We have to change how we live so we can take better care of our planet, and even possibly reverse the damage we have already done.

And you, the children of today, will be adults by the time it matters most... but you don't have to wait to be energy-smart inventors.

You can show us now how to **use energy better!**

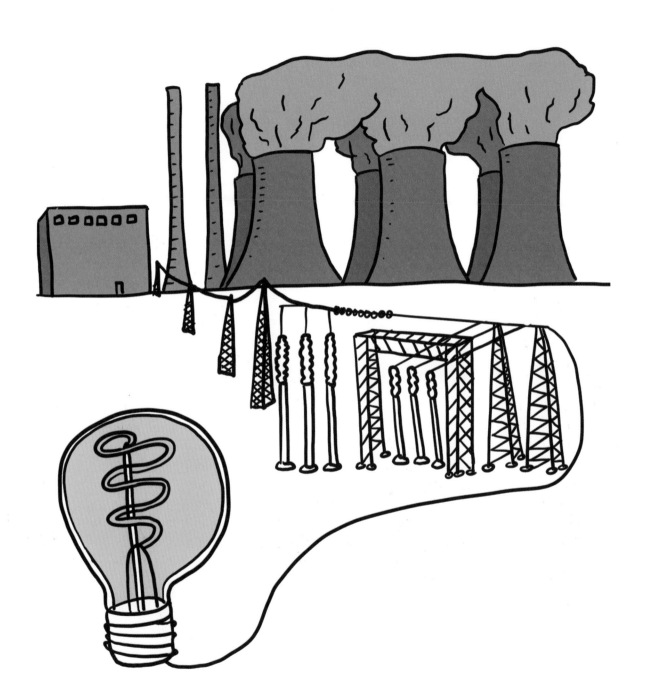

Energy makes the world go round

When cars or planes are moving, they use energy. When we turn the lights on in a room, that's energy in action.

When we move, breathe, play, think or keep our body warm, we use energy. We get our energy from food.

Energy is basically anything that makes us and the world go round!

As humans, we have always used the world around us to get energy.

Before the year 1800 we followed a **much more natural way of life** and created energy by burning natural materials such as wood, or by harnessing wind or human power!

Windmill

Hand Cart

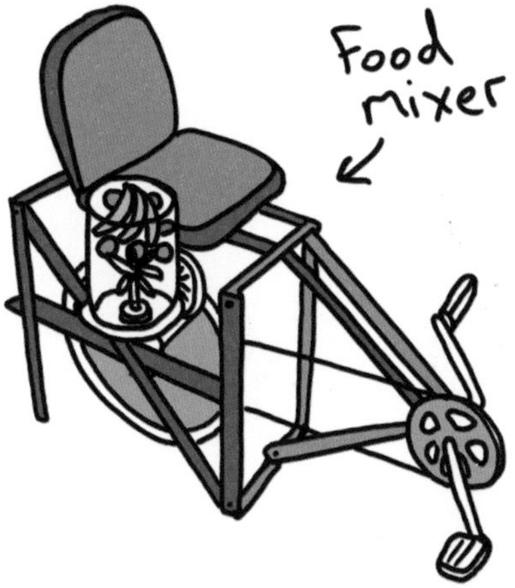

Food mixer

But over the last two centuries, our world has transformed as we have learned to make and use energy to create **new materials** and technology!

The problem is that we are still using a lot more **non-renewable energy** sources like fossil fuels than any others...

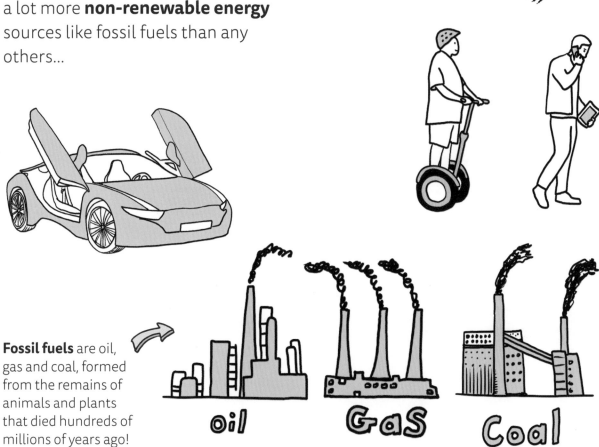

Fossil fuels are oil, gas and coal, formed from the remains of animals and plants that died hundreds of millions of years ago!

oil   GaS   Coal

To face our future energy needs, we need to transform how we create and use energy by using **renewable sources** such as...

...the sun, water, wind or even movement! So can you think of ways to create or save energy?

What movement could help?

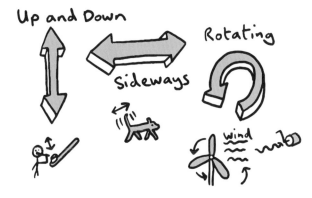

Up and Down

Sideways

Rotating

wind

How could we change the way we do everyday things?

Giant frizbee transport.

Can you think of some new ways to use renewable energy?

Turn your invention switch on!

It's time to crank up the idea factory and think about ways to make our energy future brighter and better!!! Think about...

Hamster-powered Hair dryer

Chief Inventor

Your energy inspiration

The brightest ideas are sometimes the simplest.

Use the world around you to inspire you!

My Invention!

Name it!

How it works

My Invention

Draw BIG, use colours and add labels!

Now share it on littleinventors.org!

You're SO
switched on!!

There are many things we can do to take care of our environment. But a really crucial way to address climate change is to **change how we produce, use, store and waste energy.**

This is one of the big challenges that can truly make a huge difference to our planet. We know that even little steps in the right direction can help, so let's try and take them together.

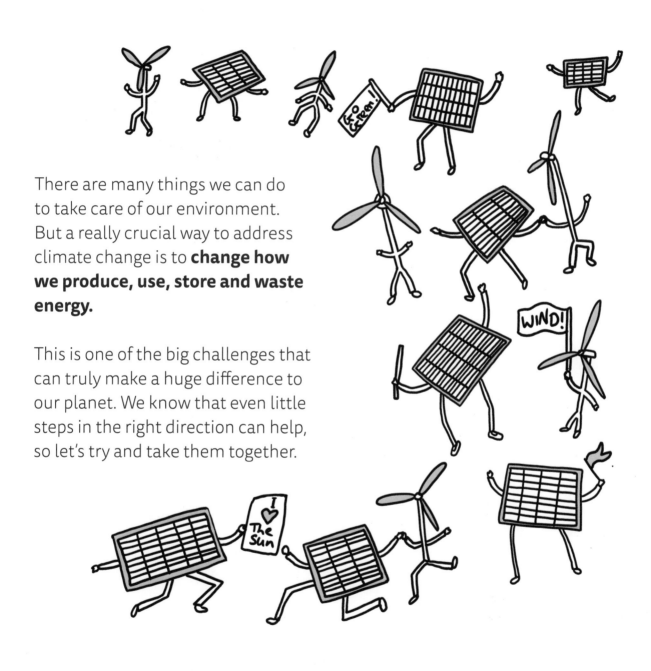

From the minds of our Little Inventors...

The band 101

Opal, age 12
Hampstead, Canada

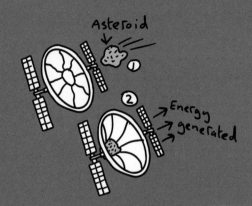

Asteroid
①
②
→ Energy
→ generated

There are so many ways that we can use energy from nature - and it can be truly out of this world!

The band 101 is a net made out of stretchy wires that conduct energy with a hole in the middle of the net. When an asteroid hits the net, it will try to go through the hole. When it succeeds, the band will lash back and the bounce creates energy that will be sent back to the space station.

Animator **Chloe Rodham** from Newcastle in the UK took on the challenge of bringing The band 101 to life by creating a model and an animation (search for **Band 101 on littleinventors.org** to see it)!

...to the skills of our Magnificent Makers

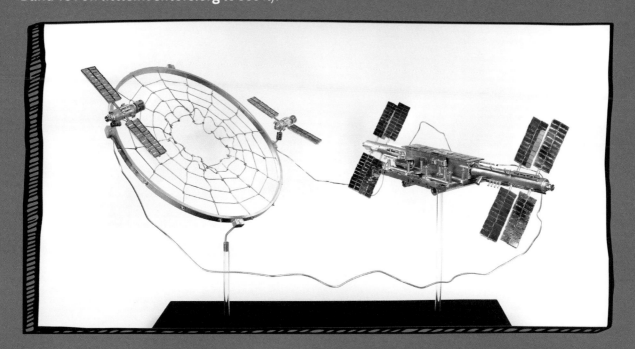

" I used lots of bits and bobs to make The band 101 – the main circle is an embroidery hoop and the solar panels are made from mosaic tiles. I made a film using stop motion animation, moving the model a small amount and photographing it each time I moved it.

" Although Opal is in a different country, we chatted over Skype and she recorded a voice-over to go with the animation, which really made it special! "

Chapter 7

What goes up must come down...

At one with the elements

We have always been fascinated by what happens above our heads.

The sky is where things that **seem impossible** take place – from birds flying effortlessly to the shimmering spectacle of the Northern Lights, from a beautiful sunrise to an infinity of stars at nighttime, the world above us is where nature really puts on the biggest show on Earth, every day!

And of course, it's not just there to entertain us...

Rain, clouds, snow, wind and more... a lot of what happens in the sky is in fact part of the **water cycle.** It's how water recycles itself. It has done so for the past 4 billion years!!

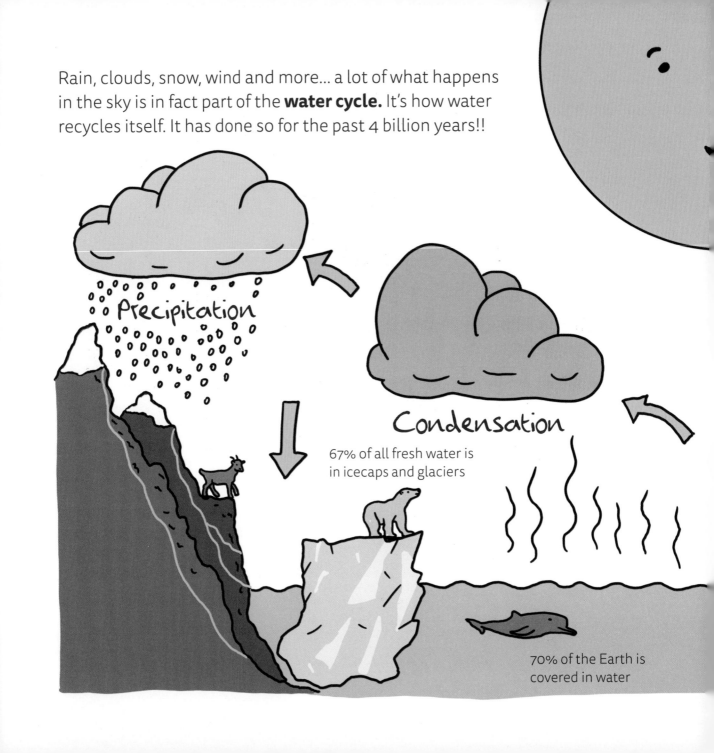

Precipitation

Condensation

67% of all fresh water is in icecaps and glaciers

70% of the Earth is covered in water

It's getting hot in here

Global warming has accelerated because of human activity. It has a very real impact on our global climate, and that affects our weather right now.

With the rise in temperatures around the planet, there are some serious effects on both the water cycle and the balance of our natural world.

As the oceans and the atmosphere get warmer, water turns to vapour faster and clouds can hold more water.

This leads to **much heavier rainfall,** less often.

Regular rainfall soaks into the ground and trickles slowly through it into rivers. But when it rains less often, the earth becomes dry and hard and heavy rain runs straight off it and into the rivers, creating **floods**. When trees, plants and grass become dry, this also means more chance of wildfires.

very dry land

Warmer oceans also mean more energy for storms, which turn into cyclones, hurricanes and typhoons.

And **glaciers** are melting and not being replaced. This means that sea level is rising, and we are losing some of our precious fresh water.

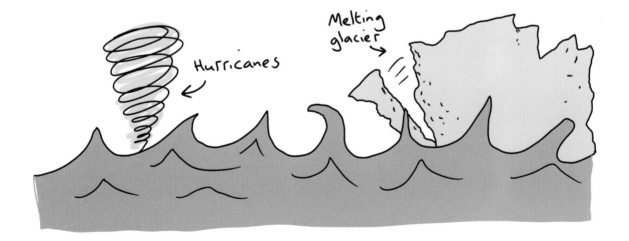

Hurricanes

Melting glacier

Time to cool down!

How could we cool the Earth down?

How could we protect or collect more fresh water?

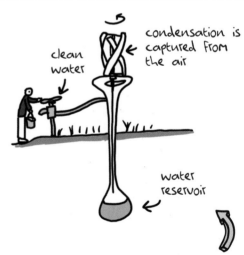

clean water

condensation is captured from the air

water reservoir

The WaterSeer is an invention that harvests water directly from the atmosphere.

If you run the tap for 2 minutes while you brush your teeth, twice a day, that's 24 litres of water used!

A single hurricane normally produces 200 times the electrical power of the whole planet in one day!!!!!

What's your hot idea for a cooler planet?

If we all put our thinking caps on, maybe we can keep our planet's ice cap on...

Chief Inventor

There is no going hot or cold when you're inventing. Let your thoughts connect freely and follow your inspiration. It can be a breeze!!

My weather inspiration!

My Invention!

Name it!

How it works

My Invention

Draw BIG, use colours and add labels!

Now share it on littleinventors.org!

Well, who's totally fresh now?

The more you know about the weather and what affects it, the more you can **make a difference** – from changing little things you do every day to thinking up really big ideas that could have a massive impact.

So maybe next time you talk about the weather, remember it's not just about the best clothes to go out in or how happy or sad it makes us!

Every form of weather is a reminder of how lucky we are to take part in this incredible adventure called life on Earth.

From the minds of our Little Inventors...

The umbrella filter

Mitchell, age 11
Halifax, Canada

When it rains, it pours... so why not get a nice glass of water out of it??

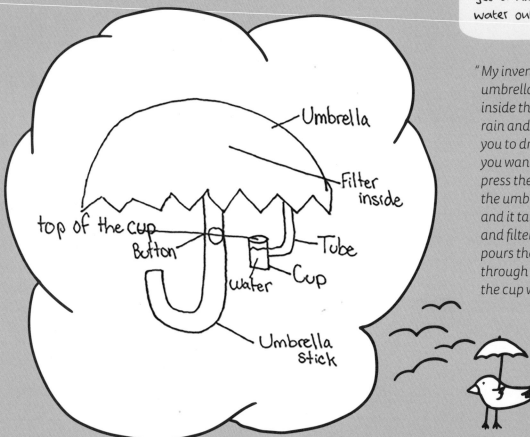

"My invention is an umbrella with a filter inside that takes rain and gives it to you to drink. When you want a drink you press the button on the umbrella stick and it takes the rain and filters it and pours the water through the tube into the cup with a straw."

The umbrella filter was made real by **Halifax Makerspace.**

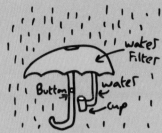

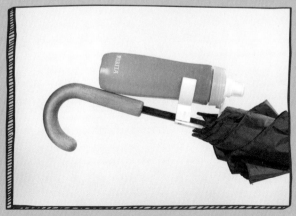

" We thought a rainwater-collecting umbrella was a very cool response to a growing problem: that of excess waste from water bottles. We love that the solution to this contemporary issue harkened back to the solution makers used to address water shortages in the past, the rain barrel...

" We used a variety of materials and techniques, including 3D design, 3D printing, sewing and woodwork to bring Mitchell's ingenious invention to life. "

Chapter 8

May the forest be with you...

Good things come in trees

Nature's superheroes!

There are over 3 trillion trees on Earth and 60,000 different species – a huge collection of colours, smells and shapes.

Trees can take hundreds of years to grow! Maybe this is why they seem so wise, strong and reliable – our most natural friends. We enjoy their shade and calm company, but there is so much more to trees than climbing up to their branches.

Trees are really hard at work, all the time! They clean the air, protect us from the sun, rain and wind, and give homes and food to birds, insects and many other animals, including us!

Their role in **keeping our planet green** is more important than ever...

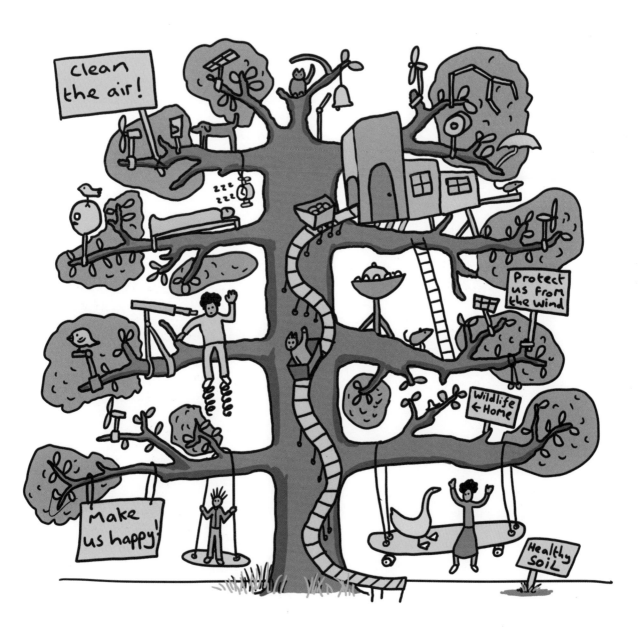

Amazing tree facts

Bird magnets!

Adding just one tree to an open space can attract up to eighty species of birds, where there were none before!

Trees have the longest lives

One of the oldest trees in the world is Methuselah in California. It's over 4,800 years old!

It was already 300 years old when the pyramids were built in ancient Egypt!

Call the tree doctor!

One large tree can produce enough oxygen in one day for four people! Doctors in Scotland are even prescribing woodland walks to help their patients heal faster...

Leonardo Da Vinci discovered that all branches of a tree put together are as thick as its trunk!!

An amazing resource

From fruit to maple syrup, and from rubber to actual wood, trees provide a variety of useful products. These are used to make rubber bands, furniture, lipstick, medicine, towels and of course paper.

Can't stand losing yew!

As cities expand, and we need more food, forests are **destroyed** to provide wood and to create space for growing crops and raising animals.

30% of the Earth's land is made up of forest. It used to be twice that, and it's predicted there might be no rainforest left in 100 years.

Right now, we are losing one football pitch of forest every SECOND!

The Amazon is the largest tropical rainforest and absorbs carbon dioxide, which is vital to climate control.

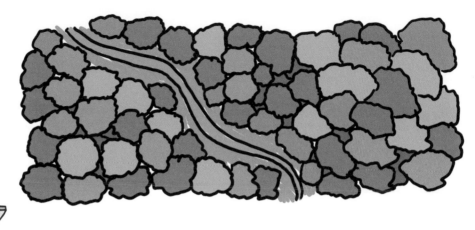

Millions of plant and animal species live in the rainforest but as it disappears, many of these are becoming extinct.

Making the planet greener by **planting more trees** is one of the simplest and best ways we can fight climate change...

Simply ash-tounding ideas!

Trees themselves are incredibly inventive living things...

Trees can talk to each other

Through their roots, trees have access to an incredible underground network made up of a special kind of fungus (from the mushroom family!). It's known as the **Wood Wide Web.**

They look after each other, like a big forest family!

Would you like some food?

Yes please send it over!

The mangrove tree is the only truly amphibious tree, living both over and under the sea, and home to birds as well as crabs!

The giant African baobab can grow to 30 metres tall and 50 metres in circumference! It's known as the **'bottle tree'** or 'tree of life' because it can store up to 120,000 litres of water!

Get barking up the right tree!!

Chief Inventor

Your invention could be inspired by all the things we can learn from trees, or by how to have more trees in our lives. You could think about ways to change how we make things so they don't use trees. It's up to you!

My tree inspiration

It can really help to let your idea take its time to grow... write it down and come back to it later and see how much it has changed! Who knows, it might even bear fruit!

Name it!

How it works

MY INVENTION

Draw BIG, use colours and add labels!

Now share it on littleinventors.org!

ExTREEordinary! You're an expert at all things tree!!

There is so much about trees to inspire ideas – how they **care** for us and the planet, how we can live in them, what we can make with them!

Trees can truly inspire us with their awesomeness! Next time you see one, just stop and think about everything it is doing, very quietly and slowly, and remember to thank it for all its mighty goodness!

We should all be more tree!!

From the minds of our Little Inventors...

Tree top

Tia, age 11
London, UK

Trees. They're about to get personal!

" The tree top is a top with trees on it. You need to water your trees once a month so they can be fresh. It is for all people but if you have trouble breathing, it is much better for you. "

...to the skills of our Magnificent Makers

Film and TV fabricator **Izy Morley** talked with Tia and John, a specialist in **hydroponics.**

" It's a way of growing plants without soil, but just with the water and food they need. So it's much easier to grow plants anywhere this way!

" In our modern cities we rarely find the time and the spaces to enjoy nature. The Tree Top is not just a fantastic idea but an important one – our air is polluted and as Tia said, breathing can be difficult. "

" After meeting with Tia and John, we settled on a stylish T-shirt with pockets and removable plants in little watering bags with nutrient-rich wadding. This way the wearer is able to grow small plants on their windowsill and wear them to suit their mood!! "

Chapter 9

Inventing for a better future...

True blue planet

Human behaviour

There are **7000 million people** on this planet.
So all the things that we do can really add up!

If we can make big or even small changes to the way we
do things, it could have a huge effect on our planet.

When we invent things, we really need to consider how
they will affect nature and our environment.

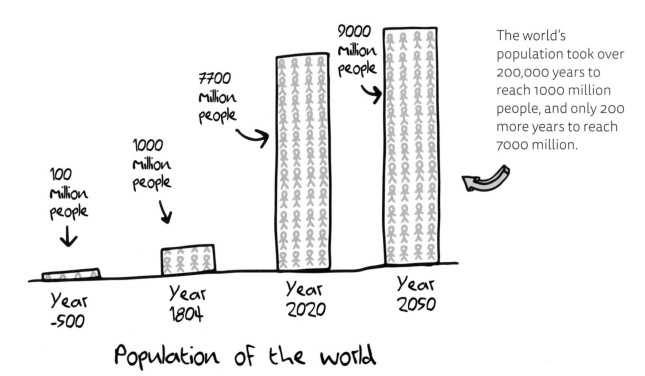

The world's population took over 200,000 years to reach 1000 million people, and only 200 more years to reach 7000 million.

100 million people

1000 million people

7700 million people

9000 million people

Year -500

Year 1804

Year 2020

Year 2050

Population of the world

Plastic bags are a recent invention, the first one being produced just over 50 years ago!

But it only takes a couple of decades for them to almost completely replace paper and cloth bags.

The **Great Pacific Garbage Patch** is discovered: an island of plastic in the middle of the ocean, mostly made of... plastic bags.

Around the world, one million new plastic bags are used every minute.

25 countries have banned plastic bags, and more continue to join the movement to beat plastic pollution...

A green planet that's mostly blue

Oceans cover 70% of the planet. We already know they are at the heart of the water cycle but that's not all. They absorb **much of the pollution** that humans produce and help keep the air cleaner.

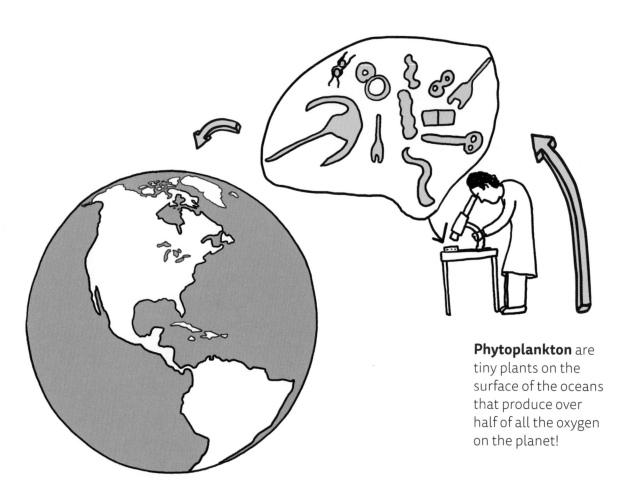

Phytoplankton are tiny plants on the surface of the oceans that produce over half of all the oxygen on the planet!

Oceans are also home to most of the life on Earth, and all these creatures, from plankton to blue whales and corals, are suffering from all the pollution coming from above the water.

Plastic

Noise pollution

Oil leak

Litter

Pollution

Shopping trolley

Chief Inventor

And on top of that, a huge amount of **plastic** and other man-made materials that we throw away ends up in the oceans too.

If we keep going as we are, **by 2050** there will be more plastic than fish in the oceans!

Amazing inventions for the future

Scientists right now are hard at work finding ways to deal with these issues...

...by making plastic bags from food waste, like cornstarch or even lobster shells!

...or making packaging out of mushrooms!

Robert Bezeau is building houses and whole villages in South America using plastic bottles!

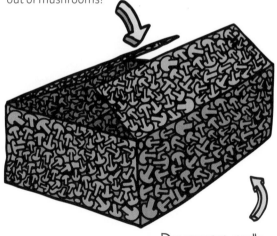

Decomposes really quickly!

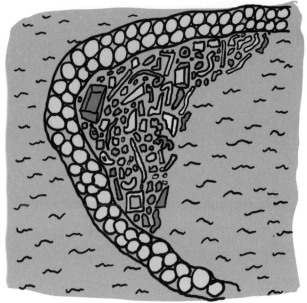

A **giant net** acts like a coastline, where plastics (even micro ones!) collect in the ocean.

Check out the Ocean Cleanup Project started by Boyan Slat when he was only 18!

Some people have even found a way to make **ink and jewellery** from air pollutants!

Invented by Dutch designer Daan Roosgaarde.

These **Supertrees** in Singapore collect rainwater and solar power, and act as vertical gardens!

Big and small ideas for serious change!

Thinking about how to help the planet can become overwhelming. Starting with little things in our everyday lives can make a big difference and lead to bigger ideas!

What can we change in our everyday lives to use less plastic?

How could you stop pollution getting into the oceans?

No more plastic bags!

A big front pocket in a jumper to carry food from the shop.

Oil leak ship with a nappy on!

Deep dive into the ocean!

Imagine what you might see under
the ocean – the good and the bad!!

Things that
shouldn't be there

What creatures can
you see underwater?

-

-

-

-

-

-

Your idea for a greener world!

Try thinking about how we could use everyday things differently, or about really big things that would truly make the world go green and keep the planet blue!

Chief Inventor

Using colour can be a great way to bring ideas to life - try using as much green as you can in your inventions, to really get inspired!

My ocean inspiration!

My Invention

Name it!

How it works

We LOVE The OCEAN

INVENT!

Ideas!

imagination!

My Invention

Draw BIG, use colours and add labels!

Now share it on littleinventors.org!

That's a massive green thumbs up to you!

We live on a beautiful planet full of extraordinary nature. We as humans are also part of this amazing collection of living beings.

If we are to keep on enjoying this incredible journey, we have to take care of our world, from the smallest bug to the really big issues, including tackling the **climate crisis.**

The good news is that there are many things that we can all do to help. Science is also at the heart of coming up with solutions that can really make a difference.

But it always starts the same way: **with ideas**.

The more ideas we all have to get to a greener planet, the more likely we are to see these ideas happen.

Magic magnet plastic catcher

Hanna, age 7
London, UK

Taking inspiration from favourite characters can open a world of ideas...

" My invention helps by catching rubbish like plastics from the water using its jagged claws, and presses the rubbish automatically so that it won't float around and pollute the ocean. Because it's on the ocean floor and can detect any live creatures, the sea will still look pretty and no sea life that lives around it will be harmed!"

Mark used pictures of Hanna to create his illustration and let her be the heroine of her own invention!

The magic magnet plastic catcher was brought to life in the form of this detailed illustration by Disney animator **Mark Henn,** who also animated Ariel, Jasmine, Tiana, Mulan and Belle!

Chapter 10

Green mind, ready to change the world...

I'm a green Little Inventor

Congratulations, you have now completed the Little Inventors go green book – you are a **Little Inventor** and ready to head out into the world and make it a greener and happier place to be!

Share your idea with the world!

We've shown you how to come up with ideas to help the planet, now it's time to share your ideas with us – and the rest of the world!

Every time you see this icon on a page,  take a picture of your invention and upload it to our website **littleinventors.org** following the easy steps online (maybe with help from a grown-up).

Your invention will be available online for all to see, plus we look at ALL the drawings we receive and love to give you personal feedback!!

And who knows, your idea could win one of our challenges and be picked to be made real!

Little Inventor, we can't wait to see your ideas!!

Taking your invention further!

You've had a brilliant invention idea, you've named it, you've drawn it... but that doesn't mean your invention journey stops there.

Our imagination doesn't stand still and inventions are the same, they can always be tweaked, improved or totally reinvented!

What's your angle?

Once you have drawn your invention, draw it again from different viewpoints.

You could do a side view but also a view from the top!

It's a great way to start taking your idea from 2D to 3D!

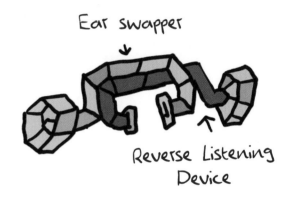

Ear swapper

Reverse Listening Device

Make a model!

Drawing is a great first step to thinking about all the different parts of your invention. The next step is to prototype it, or create a model of it. This will allow you to start thinking about it as a real object and how it might work.

You might even want to redraw your idea afterwards!

Invention 2.0

Keep your imagination going and think of your invention being used for the first time, a second time... a hundredth time.

The more we get used to something, the more we start thinking about ways to improve it.

What's your next version going to be like?

Idea buddy

Can you think of another invention that could work well?

Do your research

You have drawn your idea. But are you the first to think of it? Use the internet to search keywords to see if your invention already exists, or something close to it.

And if it does, think about how you can change it to be different and even better!

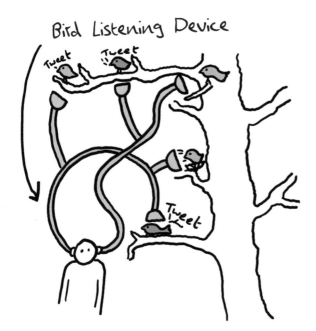

Once upon an invention...

Having an invention idea is great, but now can you think what happens next? This is your chance to write a short story about your invention idea. Think about:

Where and when it takes place...

Who are the characters in your story...

How they use the invention...

What happens as a result...

How it makes a difference...

My invention story

What do you think about your invention now? You might have discovered a new use for your invention, or decided to change it or make another one!

Inventor's log

Sometimes we have more ideas than we can handle in one go – you can't always draw ideas straight away, but you don't want to lose a good idea, do you?

List of ideas to explore later

For example: I want to invent a way to turn rubbish into food

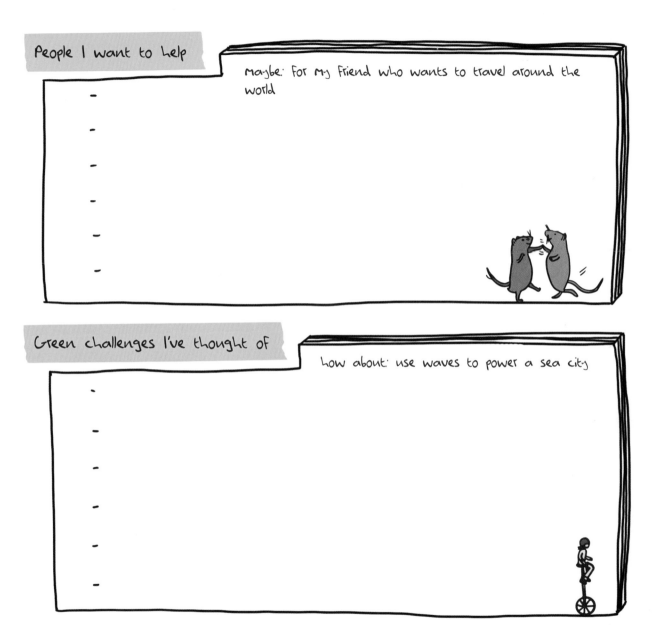

People I want to help

-
-
-
-
-
-

Maybe: For my friend who wants to travel around the world

Green challenges I've thought of

-
-
-
-
-
-

how about: use waves to power a sea city

You can download more invention sheets from **littleinventors.org** for all your ideas, plus we add new challenges all the time too!

Chapter 11

Why inventing is mighty...

Even if you're a grown-up

The power of imagination

Inventing is a natural thing for humans to do, and it starts from birth, as children discover the world on their own terms. But too often the adults in this world think that children's ideas are fanciful or plain impossible.

But if we allow ourselves to take in the full power of our children's imaginations, we open ourselves up to seeing everything around us in a fresh new way.

At Little Inventors, we believe that taking children's ideas seriously can truly make a huge difference to all of us as a society.

Creativity and **problem-solving** are qualities that all children will find essential in a future where technology and automation take care of many more of our daily tasks.

Inventing as a way to come up with solutions offers children a platform to voice their opinions and ideas. It will give them the right attitude when tackling the many challenges that lie ahead of them, both as individuals and as caring, thoughtful inhabitants of our planet (and beyond!).

Going green is something that we must all do, but you can give your children a head start. Learning to notice, respect and take care of the world and nature around them early on will most likely see them adopt greener behaviour as they become adults.

We are seeing more and more children taking action for the planet and inspiring the rest of us to stop and think about what we can do. We can learn a lot from the unrestricted imaginations of children.

Just take a few minutes to **suspend belief** and browse through their invention ideas, join in their endless curiosity and let yourself be amused, surprised or intrigued. **Thinking like a child** is likely to make you reconsider how you view your own world.

After all, it's only by challenging what we think we know that we can bring true change and progress, something that comes very naturally to our **wonderful Little Inventors.**

Top tips for grown-ups

There are some simple things you can do to help your Little Inventors feel more confident when coming up with invention ideas for a better planet:

Let them own their idea

Inventing is one of the rare occasions where children are in charge. Let them go with it!

Their world comes first

It's much easier to start inventing for people we know or for things that surround us. The big stuff will come!

Nothing is impossible

As they play with ideas, physics and reality are irrelevant, so give them the freedom to explore, with no limits.

Get informed!

Talking about the environment and the future can feel grim, but the more informed you are, the more you can help them navigate it all.

Give them the lead

Want to make your home greener? Include them in decisions about a greener home and let them take the lead to make things happen!

Go out!

There's no better way to get inspired by nature than to be out in it to let your **Little Inventors go green!**